MAMA'S PROMISES

MAMA'S PROMISES

Poems by
Marilyn Nelson Waniek

Louisiana State University Press
Baton Rouge and London   1985

Copyright © 1985 by Marilyn Nelson Waniek
All rights reserved
Manufactured in the United States of America
Designer: Joanna V. Hill
Typeface: Galliard
Typesetter: G & S Typesetters, Inc.

Library of Congress Cataloging in Publication Data

Waniek, Marilyn Nelson, 1946–
  Mama's promises.

  Includes index.
  I. Title.
PS3573.A4795M3 1985   811′.54   85-5258
ISBN 0-8071-1246-6
ISBN 0-8071-1250-X (pbk.)

Louisiana Paperback Edition, 1985
06 05 04 03 02 01 00 99 98 97 5 4 3

The paper in this book meets the guidelines for per-
manence and durability of the Committee on
Production Guidelines for Book Longevity of the
Council on Library Resources. ∞

For Mama
and for Roger and Jacob

"Life is good.
Knock on wood."
—Mama

CONTENTS

ACKNOWLEDGMENTS

Grateful acknowledgment is made to the editors of the following publications, in which some of these poems have appeared: *Callaloo, Crazyhorse, Crisis, Georgia Review, Ohio Review, Red Fox Review, Sing, Heavenly Muse!, Southern Review, 13th Moon, The William Morrow Anthology of Younger American Poets.*

I wish to thank the National Endowment for the Arts and the Yaddo Foundation for the time and quiet necessary to complete this work.

I would also like to express my gratitude to my friends Jack Davis, Pamela Espeland, and J. D. O'Hara. A special thanks to my husband, Roger B. Wilkenfeld.

MAMA'S PROMISES

A STRANGE BEAUTIFUL WOMAN

A strange beautiful woman
met me in the mirror
the other night.
Hey,
I said,
What you doing here?
She asked me
the same thing.

WILD PANSIES

for Mandy Jordan

I rested in my mother's womb,
a lily on the pond.
Gentle waves moved the water;
I rocked, held by a twisted cord
of roots.
From the moment I was planted there
I thought about learning to walk
more than nine months
before I was born.

I listened to the voices
of the water around me;
sometimes I thought a storm
was really three hearts
beating as one.

I grew from a bundle of jelly-eggs
into a tadpole nosing the water weeds.
Then I was the size of a rainbow trout,
and then I was me.

I jumped up the falls
of the birth canal
and knew, as my body
hit sunlight,
what it would feel like to fly.
But when I got to the top
I could breathe water no more.

Before I drew dry air
for the first time
into my lungs,
I said to myself, Remember.

How the pine trees
shadowed the water
when evening came.
How the sunset was reflected.
How the wild pansies
grew along the shore.

COVER PHOTOGRAPH

I want to be remembered
with big bare arms akimbo
and feet splay-toed and flat arched
on the welcome mat of dirt.

I want to be remembered
as a voice that was made to be singing
the lullaby of shadows
as a child fades into a dream.

I want to be as familiar
as the woman in the background
when the heroine is packing
and the Yankee soldiers come.

Hair covered with a bandanna,
I want to be remembered
as an autumn under maples:
a show of incredible leaves.

I want to be remembered
with breasts that never look empty,
with a child-bearing, generous waistline
and with generous, love-making hips.

I want to be remembered
with a dark face absorbing all colors
and giving them back twice as brightly,
like water remembering light.

I want to be remembered
with a simple name, like Mama:
as an open door from creation,
as a picture of someone you know.

NAMING THE ANIMAL

There's a beast in my chest,
a small totem
growing there, deep,
its feet under my tongue.
My heart is full of it;
I awake to its sound,
its unfed pacing through my sleep.
I throw out a bone,
set out a bowl of milk,
lay a full manger of clover,
but nothing is touched.

Nevertheless it's growing:
it pushes aside my veins,
it flattens my liver against my spine,
it carries a message I can't decode.
Sometimes I start to rise
and my legs don't obey.
And my eyes sometimes stare at me,
my face seems strange.

I tell myself
this will pass
but I lie so badly
awake at night,
staring at the ceiling's stars.

It's growing into my body's old dress,
my soul's worn shoes,
my kid glove of skin
and I still don't know
if the opening pupils
I find in the mirror
are a tiger's, or a sheep's.

HERBS IN THE ATTIC

A cat by the fireside, purring.
But I don't stop there; I go
through the living room and up the stairs.
My little brother stirs in his crib.
My sister and I sleep in our tumbled rooms,
and our parents sleep together,
fingers intertwined.

The second stairway's narrow.
It darkens when I close the door
behind me. And I climb up to the attic,
to the bustles and pantaloons
hidden in trunks, the diaries and love letters,
the photographs, the rings,
the envelopes full of hair.

Here's the old silverware
Great Aunt Irene and Uncle Eric used.
Her fork is curved
from her lifelong habit
of scraping the plate.
His knife is broader,
the better to butter his bread.

Here are the bookcases of Tarzan,
Zane Grey, a textbook Shakespeare,
piles of *National Geographic*, *Look*, and *Life*.

I sit on the dusty floor
and open a book.
Dream music fills the air
like the scent of dried herbs.

MY SECOND BIRTH

That first birth
when I pushed myself
free of her
and burst out
into invisible air
is as lost to me
as the months I floated
in that ocean of unbroken thought.

But passing on
the birth she gave me
has made me see Mama
face to face.

I understand now
what she means when she says
she loves me:
It's the place you get to
when you've pushed
to the other side of pain.

A light grew in my belly
until my husband
could warm his hands by it.
I gave our son my broken sleep,
the fists, hands, fists, hands, fists
I made when he woke me
from my dream about his name.

I gave birth to him awed
by his apple-round head
in the bright glass above my knees.
I was given new strength
when he crowned
and my blood burst
like a chain of jewels
around his neck.

Mama
was my first image of God.
I remember how she leaned over my crib,
her eyes full of sky.

THE DANGEROUS CARNIVAL

One of the signs of a concussion
is dilated pupils. My son's pupils
dilate whenever he sees me.
The top of his skull
is a breastbone of paper.
I pace through the child-proofed house
and pray that he'll wake.

My life these days
is a dangerous carnival.
No wonder I pinned his blankets to him,
hid him for safe-keeping
under the water of the pond.
Hungry eyes watch me walk the midway
past their rickety cages. For a dime
you can shoot at a skyful of women
in shorts and jogging shoes, or stand
at the back of the sweaty crowd
in the tent of THE FEROCIOUS BABY,
the BABY with VAMPIRE TEETH,
who sucked its mother's breasts so hard
she DISAPPEARED ONE NIGHT IN HER BED.

Someone recognizes me, shouts
in the pulsating rape of garish lights.
I want to run, but the baby's an anvil,
my breasts are concrete blocks,
I stagger under the weight.
In the getaway car the baby claws
at my hands; I fight to keep the wheels
on a track that bends back on itself,
its walls so steep the tires scream and scream.

I can't go on.
There's too much to do.
I can't keep up.
Somewhere behind me
someone is crying.
He's alive!
I have to take him his breast.

The blank picture windows
make this a room of trick mirrors:
as I rush to pick him up
I see a pigtailed little girl,
arms held wide for balance,
in Mama's size 10 high-heeled shoes.

MAMA'S PROMISE

I have no answer to the blank inequity
of a four-year-old dying of cancer.
I saw her on t.v. and wept
with my mouth full of meatloaf.

I constantly flash on disasters now;
red lights shout *Warning. Danger.*
everywhere I look.
I buckle him in, but what if a car
with a grille like a sharkbite
roared up out of the road?
I feed him square meals
but what if the fist of his heart
should simply fall open?
I carried him safely
as long as I could,
but now he's a runaway
on the dangerous highway.
Warning. Danger.
I've started to pray.

But the dangerous highway
curves through blue evenings
when I hold his yielding hand
and snip his miniscule nails
with my vicious-looking scissors.
I carry him around
like an egg in a spoon,
and I remember a porcelain fawn,
a best friend's trust,
my broken faith in myself.
It's not my grace that keeps me erect
as the sidewalk clatters downhill
under my rollerskate wheels.

Sometimes I lie awake
troubled by this thought:
It's not so simple to give a child birth;
you also have to give it death,
the jealous fairy's christening gift.

I've always pictured my own death
as a closed door,
a black room,
a breathless leap from the mountain top
with time to throw out my arms, lift my head,
and see, in the instant my heart stops,
a whole galaxy of blue.
I imagined I'd forget,
in the cessation of feeling,
while the guilt of my lifetime floated away
like a nylon nightgown,
and that I'd fall into clean, fresh forgiveness.

Ah, but the death I've given away
is more mine than the one I've kept:
from my hand the poisoned apple,
from my bow the mistletoe dart.

Then I think of Mama,
her bountiful breasts.
When I was a child, I really swear,
Mama's kisses could heal.
I remember her promise,
and whisper it over my sweet son's sleep:

> *When you float to the bottom, child,*
> *like a mote down a sunbeam,*
> *you'll see me from a trillion miles away:*
> *my eyes looking up to you,*
> *my arms outstretched for you like night.*

THE LOST DAUGHTER

One morning just before Christmas
when I was four or five years old
I followed Mama's muskrat coat
and her burgundy cloche
from counter to counter in The May Co.
as she tested powders and colognes,
smoothed silk scarves and woolen vests,
and disappeared down the aisle
into the life she lived before I was born.

The mirrors rendered nothing more
at my eye level than a small brown blur;
I understood why the salesclerks didn't see
a little girl in a chesterfield coat,
plaid bows on her five skimpy braids,
or stop me as I wept my way
toward the outside doors
and was spun through their transparency
out into the snow.

On the sidewalk Santa rang a shiny bell
and shifted from his right boot to his left
as the fingers in my mittens froze
and fell off, one by one.
My skin, then my bones turned to stone
that parted the hurrying crowd,
until at last I drifted, thinned as the smoke
from an occasional pipe or cigarette,
through the thick white words people spoke.

Sometimes a taxi squealed its brakes
or beeped to pierce the solid, steady roar
of voices, wheels, and motors.
The same blue as the sky by now,
I rose like a float in the parade
I'd seen not long before:
a mouse tall as a department store
that nodded hugely as it moved
above our wonder down the avenue.

When Mama spat out my name
in fury and relief, I felt my face
fly back into focus. I formed again
instantaneously under her glaring eyes.
In the plate glass window I recognized
the shape Mama shook and embraced—
the runny nose, the eyes' frightened gleam,
the beret askew on hair gone wild—
and knew myself made whole again, her child.

THE MARRIAGE NIGHTMARE

He's so romantic he's kissed both my arms
past the elbows; now he's nibbling my neck
in a motel room with pictures of kittens
on each of its dingy white walls.
He turns away to open
that odd-shaped affair on the bed,
and withdraws a tenor sax.
He plays mellow jazz as I shimmy
out of my clothes and slip between the sheets.
Then he lays it on the dresser,
pulls his sweater over his head.
The coarse black hair around his navel
leaves me breathless and oozy.
He smiles, unbuckles his belt,
and my husband bursts into the room.

I wake up to a blue day.
Downstairs my husband and child
have already eaten breakfast.
The Sunday *Times* is scattered,
greasy, sprinkled with crumbs.
I sit in my nightgown at the table,
my head still frowsy.
My child whines against my knee;
if I concentrate hard enough
I can ignore him.
My husband demands to know
why I'm so sullen.
If I concentrate hard enough
maybe he'll go away.
The child's whining grows;
he throws the book he wants me to read.
My husband grabs him and storms out.
The door slams behind them.

I hear five smacks.
The child screams.
Then the door slams again
and my husband stands before me,
bigger than usual.
I wake up to a blue day.

LEVITATION WITH BABY

The Muse bumped
against my window this morning.
No one was at home but me
and the baby. The Muse said
there was room on her back for two.
Okay, I said, *but first I've got to*

Pack his favorite toys.
Small ones are the best:
that way he can sit and play quietly
as the earth slides out from under our feet.
Let's see, somewhere there's
a wind-up dog with a drum
that sometimes keeps him busy
ten minutes or more.
And we'd better take some books.

Disposable diapers,
pre-moistened towelettes,
plastic bags,
and I'll pack a lunch.
Peanut butter and crackers
are nutritious,
and the crumbs brush right off.

While I was packing his lunch
the baby got hungry,
so I put him in his high chair,
unpacked the crackers,
and gave him some.
He threw the third one down,
so I took him out,
wiped the high chair,

wiped the floor under and around the chair,
wiped the window next to it,
and wiped his fingers and face.
Then I took off his pants,
shook them out,
and wiped the soles of his shoes.

I filled two plastic bottles,
changed his diaper,
and got him dressed.
I washed my hands.
I sat down at my desk.
Okay, I said. *Now*
I'm ready for takeoff.

As he cried for a bottle
I saw my next-door neighbor,
shirtless, in the pants he wears
to work in his garden,
scribbling furiously on the back of a paper bag
as he ascended over the roof of his house
on the Muse's huge, sun-spangled wings.

IT'S ALL IN YOUR HEAD

for Deborah M.

How easily my heart falls back into habits:
a little stress, and I'm checking my pulse again
for irregular beats.
Just last year I went once a week
to the emergency room,
afraid my breath would expand
the radiant pain in my chest.
I lay among the hurt, the dying,
checking my symptoms off on a mental list.

I didn't die; I napped
on the spotless stainless steel beds.
I went home chastened, humble,
to the steeplechase of my life.
Now, like a bass drum dropped down the stairs,
my heart wakes me up again at night.
I pretend I'm not afraid
as the funeral procession
comes to order under my ribs.

I wanted to twirl a baton
in the Twenty Eighty-five parade.
The day Mrs. Gray said I'd be famous,
the sixth grade class dissolved
to an image of high-stepping white boots.
But now I stumble after, out of step,
as the band strikes up a hymn
and the colored congregation
slowly begins to move.

The trombone fades in the distance
with the flattened-out trumpets and drums;
my ancestors carry black parasols:
Diverne, Annie, Ray, Mary, Charlie.
Geneva, Oneida, Zilphia, Blanche,
in shabby shoes and black straw hats
rescued from the backs of their closets.
Dark dresses reserved for such occasions
flicker around their calves.

Their felt fedoras in their hands,
their collars too white,
their heads small
with new haircuts, my grandfathers
and uncles walk in the bright morning.
Pete has taken off his apron,
John, his overalls. Melvin, Rufus, Pomp,
in shiny shoes and suits, march
with Mister Tyler and the women.

I limp behind in my black hole shoes,
my hair crocheted with tangles
as it was when I was ten.
My old heart groans
when the brass light from the tuba
takes the road that winds up the hill.
I hear the sisters ahead of me
join in a church-house moan
as the band ascends into the blues.

The moan changes
to a melody vaguely familiar,
though they're too far away now
for me to hear more than snatches.
I hum along with them,
halting and out of sync,
like a jay
in a tree full of finches.

It's jazz I hear now from the heights,
hands clap a rhythm like approaching rain.
I want to be a part of that music,
but I fall back again and again,
damned impossible stone.
By the time I pant up the narrow ridge
only the thin voice of a clarinet
rises from small blacks and lights.

It's too soon for me to follow them over
from the top of my birth date
to the other side of the dash,
where I'll be welcomed with fanfare.
This syncopation's only a habit
my heart has picked up.
So I march back home
to the business
of putting on diapers
and taking them off.

WOMEN'S LOCKER ROOM

The splat of bare feet on wet tile
breaks the incredible luck
of my being alone in here.
I snatch a stingy towel
and sidle into the shower. I'm already soaped
by the time a white hand turns the neighboring knob.
I recognize the arm as one that flashed
for many rapid laps while I dogpaddled at the shallow end.
I dart an appraising glance: She arches down
to wash her lifted heel, and is beautiful.
As she straightens, I look into her eyes.

For an instant I remember human sacrifice:
The female explorer led skyward,
her blond tresses loose on her neck;
the drums of our pulses grew louder;
I raised the obsidian knife.
Violets bloomed in the clefts of the stairs.

I could freeze her name in an ice cube,
bottle the dirt from her footsteps
with potent graveyard dust.
I could gather the combings from her hairbrush
to burn with her fingernail clippings,
I could feed her Iago powder.
Childhood taunts, branded ears,
a thousand insults swirl through my memory
like headlines in a city vacant lot.

I jump, grimace, divide like an amoeba
into twin rages that stomp around
with their lips stuck out,
then come suddenly face to face.
They see each other and know that they
are mean mamas.
Then I bust out laughing
and let the woman live.

CONFESSIONAL POEM

This friend of mine
says she'd like to visit
the lonely young mother she's seen
in a fourth floor window.
She'd climb the unswept stairs
and whisper a word,
the locks would click,
and the apartment door would open.

There, in the overheated air
and the turbulence of children,
she'd stand, the Fat Lady suit
hanging from her shoulders
like a sandwich board.

She'd strip off
the fake rabbit coat—a good buy—
and dance around in the bargain basement
housedress. She'd undo the dress snap
by snap, all the while eyeing the youngest baby
eyeing the doorway to the john.
Under the housedress she'd wear
a black nylon slip
with a side seam ripped out.

She says she'd wiggle wiggle the hips
and wink at no one in particular
as the oldest baby pulled the middle baby's hair
and the youngest disappeared through the bathroom doorway.
She'd raise the slip like an opera curtain,
ripple the cellulite thighs,
and shimmy her shoulders
to open the diaper pin
closing the back of the bra.

By now the young mother
would have left the sooty window;
she'd sit laughing on the sofa,
jiggling a baby on her knees.

And my friend says she'd dance,
in the Zeppelin glory of the melony breasts,
the magnificent girth, the silver and auburn
stretch marks on the belly
like a night of Northern Lights.
She'd lift her arms and twirl
like a ballerina,
then swing her elbows and tap like a dancing fool.
Heavy and beautiful, the young mother would get up
and join her, her pregnancy big
as an extra silhouette.
In the faint cloud of dust they raised
the middle baby would bend and straighten its knees,
dancing in its heavy diaper; the oldest
would throw back its head and whirl, whirl.
From the bathroom the youngest,
hearing laughter, would leave a wet trail,
then sit up and clap happy hands.

Then I'd strip off
the Fat Lady suit
and dance on, like a blaze of sunlight.

SLEEPLESS NIGHTS

We used to tell each other erotic stories
at slumber parties when I was about ten:
We'd meet and kiss dark, handsome boys,
and then sink into sixty-year dreams
from which we'd wake up for church weddings
and to name our butterscotch babies.
From there we always jumped ahead
to the pooping-out party, and died laughing
into our silencing pillows at the way
we'd overdose on laxatives, and be dead.

We never dreamed of the face-making
self-reconstruction from scratch
we'd be engaged in for most of our lives,
of at thirty-four an ordinary day
on which an aspiration is adjusted down
another notch like a dress let out twice
at the waist, then finally given away,
of the rambling Victorian responsibilities we'd own,
full of furniture that doesn't match
and appliances that always need kicking.

We carefully flushed away the traces
of the filched cigarettes we'd tried
before our two o'clock forays in the dark,
then we raced back on tiptoe to devour
unsweetened chocolate, olives, laundry starch,
and in our floppy pajamas, giggled for hours.

When we made out each others' drawn faces
by the first pale murmurs of light
we were stupefied
to see how old we could grow overnight.

SORT OF A CALLING

Under a yellow moon that mused
over Hartford's insurance towers
and the red, white, and black of the road,
I drove home on the last night in November
and thought about money. At home my son
asked me to sit by his bed until he slept.
I sat in the darkened room and thought
about money. In bed beside
my husband's comfortable breath,
I lay awake for what seemed like hours,
figuring out ways to pay Peter and Paul,
trying to forgive my creditors.

Guilt rules my waking hours
like a military tyrant.
Thou shalt not sin
so much against the poor,
it insists, giving me a list
of *isms* any decent person
should have the good sense
to resist. I despise self-righteousness,
but I sweated in my hair pajamas.

And I called on all the powers
to bring back my dead, looked for them
under beds with a flashlight,
searched through strange Victorian houses.
As usual, home was a carousel
whose redblueyellow horses were a blur
I could hardly decipher.

The mantras of my everyday life
refuse to blend
into a name I can call
to hush the voices I can't escape
into a single voice in the wind,
but I lay awake, anyway,
inventing incantations
to call up and hold back
the pre-Christmas light over Hartford,
the yellowish tint in a black student's skin,
the smooth efficiency of my car, the full moon,
the trees near my house that embraced me
in their familiar shadow, my husband's welcoming face
looking up from the checkbook, our son's voice piping
"Mama, you came home!" and starting to sing.

MAMA'S MURDERS

Her leg flies open like a dictionary dropped,
the white fat sickens till her blood
fills the wound, and I, dumb with terror,
run away from the gully gaudy with broken glass
while my sister's scream shrinks to child size
at my cowardly back. A white door opens
as my fists blur on the wood.
The white lady who takes me in
has no age, has no face, only a voice
from somewhere else that asks my mother's name
over the rip of clean sheets.
Jennifer comes alone up the forbidden trail,
leaving bloody footprints in the snow.

Five-fifty on a wet October morning.
I'm awake now, still running home to get Mama,
confession still cold on my tongue.
I sit up in the dark. I count my murders.
    My brother died, a brown leaf
    against a wire fence.
    My father never got to say goodbye.
    The boy who gave his mouth to me
    saw death in the rear-view mirror,
    turned around to meet it, met it.

Because I daydreamed about how beautiful I'd be
with tears in my eyes.
Because I didn't throw myself over a grenade.
Because of my stupid fault.
How many more have I watched,
helpless, pulled over the falls?

I might have saved them,
might have torn off my senior prom gown
and dived into the torrent.
In front of my horrified eyes
they went over without a sound
like a herd of stampeding cattle
crazy with thirst.
Bloody boys, broken women,
thin children,
I might have saved them.

As dawn colors the sky
with sad gray radiance
I count the day I ran to tell Mama
we broke Jamie Crowl's arm on the seesaw,
the day I ran to tell Mama I made Jennifer
take the dangerous shortcut from school,
the day I ran to tell Mama my voodoo had worked.

I remember how she fed me Cheerios
while the news announced in a cold white voice
the numbers of the dead.
How she watched me pore over photographs
of mountains of eyeglasses, mountains of shoes,
then sent me out to play
in the twilight under the streetlamps;
how Junebugs fell heavy and horrible
under my flying feet.

I hear my baby waking up,
trying out my new name like a chant.
Before I face his wonderful eyes
I slip into my raggedy robe
and wash my hands and face.

In the mirror I look like Mama.
I lean closer and look into her eyes:
In their black pupils, I see my grandmother,
her mother, diminishing generations
of the dead, all of them Mama.

I, too, have given my child
to the murderous world.
I go to him, pick him up,
feel in my chest like warm liquid
hundreds of generations of Mama's forgiveness.

LIGHT UNDER THE DOOR

I remember hiding in the hall closet,
down with the dust and the extra shoes,
the hems of the big people's coats
brushing my uppermost braids. Daddy was coming.
I could tell from the crunch of wheels,
the thunk of the heavy car door,
the rattle of keys at the lock.
His hard-soled shoes came toward me,
a voice like Othello's
asked my mother where I was.
I was ready to swoon with delight,
but the footsteps faded,
the voice asked for dinner.

I remember the smell of wool,
the gritty floor under my palms,
the thin light under the door.
My mother stirred, chopped,
opened the oven to check on the cornbread.
I heard her answer my sister
while Daddy went into their bedroom
to take off his Air Force uniform.
Outside, a plane like a buzz saw
sliced the distant sky.

That day in kindergarten
a buzzer went off;
Mrs. Liebel jumped up
and made us hide on the polished floor
under our desks.
Not even the naughty boys giggled
as we watched a fly explore
the alphabet over the blackboard
and looked up at wads of petrified gum.
I'm sitting in the closet now,
waiting for the bomb.

No, that's a lie.
I'm standing here in the kitchen,
a grown up woman, a mother,
with used breasts. Upstairs,
the man I love and our son
are playing. The baby
touches his father's knee,
steps, stops, then runs away
with his off-balance gait.
His father chases him, hooting,
to the table where they stop for breath,
then the baby squeals and takes off
for the other room.

The sun rises in the window over the breakfast table
as I scramble the eggs. On the radio
a pleasant male voice announces yesterday's
disasters. The jays have carried the larger crumbs off,
now they come back for the rest.

My father opened the closet door. A light like a look
into the heart of fire blinded me for a moment:
I didn't see him there.
I remember the good smell of beans and cornbread
and the clash of plates being put on the table.
I remember Mama's voice humming mezzo
as I walked out into the light.

BALI HAI CALLS MAMA

As I was putting away the groceries
I'd spent the morning buying
for the week's meals I'd planned
around things the baby could eat,
things my husband would eat,
and things I should eat
because they aren't too fattening,
late on a Saturday afternoon
after flinging my coat on a chair
and wiping the baby's nose
while asking my husband
what he'd fed it for lunch
and whether
the medicine I'd brought for him
had made his cough improve,
wiping the baby's nose again,
checking its diaper,
stepping over the baby
who was reeling to and from
the bottom kitchen drawer
with pots, pans, and plastic cups,
occasionally clutching the hem of my skirt
and whining to be held,
I was half listening for the phone
which never rings for me
to ring for me
and someone's voice to say that
I could forget about handing back
my students' exams which I'd had for a week,
that I was right about *The Waste Land*,
that I'd been given a raise,
all the time wondering
how my sister was doing,
whatever happened to my old lover(s),
and why my husband wanted
a certain brand of toilet paper;
and I wished I hadn't, but I'd bought
another fashion magazine that promised

to make me beautiful by Christmas,
and there wasn't room for the creamed corn
and every time I opened the refrigerator door
the baby rushed to grab whatever was on the bottom shelf
which meant I constantly had to wrestle
jars of its mushy food out of its sticky hands
and I stepped on the baby's hand and the baby was screaming
and I dropped the bag of cake flour I'd bought to make cookies
    with
and my husband rushed in to find out what was wrong because
    the baby
was drowning out the sound of the touchdown although I had
    scooped
it up and was holding it in my arms so its crying was inside
my head like an echo in a barrel and I was running cold water
on its hand while somewhere in the back of my mind wondering
    what
to say about *The Waste Land* and whether I could get away with
    putting
broccoli in a meatloaf when

suddenly through the window
came the wild cry of geese.

DINOSAUR SPRING

A violet wash is streaked across the clouds.
Triceratops, Brachiosaurus, Trachodon
browse the high greenery, heave through
the dissipating mists.
They are as vacant as we are:
They don't see how mountains are growing,
how flowers change spring by spring,
how feathers form.

Last night I walked among the dinosaurs,
hardly taller than a claw.
I touched their feet with my fingertips,
my tongue numb with wonder.

At seven this morning two mallards
and a pair of Canada geese
preened themselves in the light of the pond.
Awake on a morning like this one,
jays screeching from treetop to fencepost,
I have to strain to imagine
how people wake up
in San Salvador, in Cape Town, in Beirut.
The background roar grows louder,
a neighbor screams for her child.

Just now I took my baby out of his crib
and teetered on the edge of the vortex.
I saw millions of hands imploring,
mouths open, eyes his.
I fell into a universe of black, starry water,
and through that into monstrous love
that wants to make the world right.

I can comfort my son:
The ghost in the closet, the foot-eating fish
on the floor can be washed away
with a hug and a tumbler of milk.
But the faceless face? The nuclear piñata
over our heads? The bone finger pointing?

Through the window I see the sky
that hung over the dinosaurs.
The flight of a grackle catches my eye
and pulls it down toward the moving water.
I can't see the larger motion, leaves
moldering into new soil.
If I lay on my back in the yard,
I'd feel how we're hanging on
to this planet, attached even to her
by the sheer luck of gravity.

I have to shake my head, I've grown so solemn.
It's my turn to vacuum the house.
In the din, I go back to my dream:
Holding my son by the hand,
I walk again among the dinosaurs.
In my breast my heart pours and pours
so that it terrifies me, pours and pours out
its fathomless love, like the salt mill
at the bottom of the sea.

THE CENTURY QUILT

for Sarah Mary Taylor, Quilter

My sister and I were in love
with Meema's Indian blanket.
We fell asleep under army green
issued to Daddy by Supply.
When Meema came to live with us
she brought her medicines, her cane,
and the blanket I found on my sister's bed
the last time I visited her.
I remembered how I'd planned to inherit
that blanket, how we used to wrap ourselves
at play in its folds and be chieftains
and princesses.

Now I've found a quilt
I'd like to die under;
Six Van Dyke brown squares,
two white ones, and one square
the yellowbrown of Mama's cheeks.
Each square holds a sweet gum leaf
whose fingers I imagine
would caress me into the silence.

I think I'd have good dreams
for a hundred years under this quilt,
as Meema must have, under her blanket,
dreamed she was a girl again in Kentucky
among her yellow sisters,
their grandfather's white family
nodding at them when they met.
When their father came home from his store
they cranked up the pianola
and all of the beautiful sisters
giggled and danced.
She must have dreamed about Mama
when the dancing was over:
a lanky girl trailing after her father
through his Oklahoma field.

Perhaps under this quilt
I'd dream of myself,
of my childhood of miracles,
of my father's burnt umber pride,
my mother's ochre gentleness.
Within the dream of myself
perhaps I'd meet my son
or my other child, as yet unconceived.
I'd call it The Century Quilt,
after its pattern of leaves.

I SEND MAMA HOME

I send you down the road from Paden
scaring bobwhites and pheasants
back into the weeds;
a jackrabbit keeps pace
in front of your headlights
if you drive there at night.
I send you to Boley
past a stand of post oaks
and the rolling blackjack hills.

On Pecan Street
a brown rectangle outlines the spot
where King's Ice House used to be.
The Farmer's and Merchant's Bank
is closed, grizzled boards
blind its windows.
The ghosts of Mister Turner,
the murdered banker,
and Floyd Birdwell,
the right hand of Pretty Boy Floyd,
spill like shadows
over the splintering floor.

This was the city of promise,
the town where no white man
showed his face after dark.
The *Progress* extolled it
in twice weekly headlines
as "Boley, the Negro's Dream."

Mama, I give you this poem
so you can drive past
Hazel's Department Store,
Bragg's Barber Shop,
the Truelove Cafe,
the Antioch Baptist Church,
the C.M.E. church and school,
the Creek-Seminole college.

I deliver you again
to your parents' bedroom
where the piano gleamed
like a black pegasus,
to the three-room farmhouse,
to the Oklahoma plains.
I give you the horses, Prince and Lady,
and the mules. I give you your father's car,
a Whippet, which you learned to drive
at a slow bounce through the pasture.
I give you the cows and calves
you and your brother played rodeo on,
the full smokehouse, the garden,
the fields of peanuts and cotton.

I send you back
to the black town you missed
when you were at college
and on the great white way.
I let you see
behind the mask you've worn
since the fifty-year-ago morning
when you waved goodbye from the train.

I DREAM THE BOOK OF JONAH

for Mel Nelson and Pamela Espeland

I fell asleep on the couch

One stormy April afternoon
While Roger and Jacob were shopping
I lay down on the couch and had a dream.

Lord, Lord, sang Jonah
Trouble on my mind
Lord, sweet Mama,
Trouble on my mind.
If you love me like you tell me,
Why don't you give a sign?

Jonah began his story

Well, God wakes me up from a nap on the couch
and a dream of talking to an angel,
and says
GET READY TO LEAVE IN TEN MINUTES FOR NINEVAH.
I'd heard of it once
when I was a kid,
and what I remembered wasn't pretty:
fast women on drugs,
kids rapin old ladies,
lonesome men sittin all day at the movies
with their pants unzipped.
Not this boy, I says,
and I heads out in the opposite direction,
out towards Tarshish, a city I visited one time
back durin the war.

A lot of funny things happen on the way to the port.
First an oak tree blows down
most on top of me.
Lucky for me I jumped back real quick,
but a bolt of lightnin just missed,
and the sky was a shotgun
spittin out hail
when I got to the ship.

It was stormin like crazy,
and the weather got worse.
I was soppin. The deck
was all slippery with puke.
I prayed on my knees
to a sky white with thunder,
and the other men hears me
and blames it all on me.
They says, Man look what happens
when you try to slip away from God.

Then they grabs my cash
and throws me overboard.

Then Jonah took out his guitar

Well, I was tryin to swim,
which was hard to begin with,
when the biggest old fish in the world
looms up like a freight train out of the fog.
I thought I was done for.

It was no picnic in that fish's belly.
It was hot in the first place,
and it stunk to high heaven.
There was nothing to eat,
nothin to hold on to,
nothin to breathe
but what felt like squids.
I was in there for days,
but it felt like a lifetime.
I kept my mouth up out of the slime
and I prayed like a preacher.

I woke up on a beach somewhere,
thirsty as hell.
I was glad to be alive,
I'll admit,
but I was hoppin mad.

Now Jonah began to tune his guitar

Well, the next thing I know,
here comes God again,
saying, I TOLD YOU NINEVAH.
AND LET THIS BE A WARNING TO YOU.
Well, this time I went.

I spent a day or two walkin around,
sort of gettin the feel of the place.
It was like walkin in shit.
(Excuse me, ladies.)
I figure God's right:
this place should be cleaned up.

After a while I stops walkin.
I puts my hat on the sidewalk,
and I starts in to sing.
A crowd forms around me:
a bunch of shriveled up women
out lookin through they glasses
at the window displays.
When I sing out God's warnin to Ninevah,
they like to jump out they skins.
They leave quick and come back
with they fancy-dressed sons,
they skinny-legged daughters
and they gun-totin men.

I can see they eyes
narrow to hate me,
and then, as I pick up the beat,
they eyes widen with fear.
Pretty soon the street in front of me,
the main street, and all of the other
busy streets in town
was full of people on they knees,
swayin and cryin and prayin
to the melody of my song.

For the next thirty days
everbody in Ninevah but me,
right on down to the lap dogs,
went without eatin.

I ate porkchops and lobsters every night.
In empty restaurants.
Alone.

And Jonah began to stroke a tentative rhythm

After a month or so,
I goes up to a hilltop
and waits.

I waits about a week.

If it hadn't a been for some country folks
on they way into Ninevah for a good time,
I could of starved.

After a while I gets fed up with waitin.
I asks God why She was holdin things up,
and God says, GRACE.
Meaning mercy, I think.

I says, What?
You mean I did all that singin for nothin?
Them people is gone to be laughin off they heads!

All this trouble,
I says,
and you changed your mind?

I just wanted to die.

Now his fingers found the melody

Well, I goes out in the desert
and I sits in the sun.

Hot enough to fry lizards!

Then somethin shoots out the sand
right beside me, like a geyser,
tall as a tree.

It was a tree.
I was catchin my breath
and feelin the place in my neck
where the pulse is
when God's voice says,
RELAX. ENJOY.
So I sit in the shade.

That night I dream
about tellin my friends
how God made me a miracle
in Ninevah.
I wake up with a splittin headache,
layin right out in the sun.
The tree's just a handful of ashes.

I jumps to my feet.
Hey, that was a wonderful tree!
I yells, talkin to heaven
and kickin the sand.
Who do you think you are?

Then a voice booms so close to me
it could a been inside my head.
WHO DO YOU THINK I AM? it says.
I MADE THE TREE, AND NINEVAH,
AND YOU.
WHO THE HELL YOU THINK
YOU TALKIN TO?

So Jonah sang the blues

Lord, Lord, sweet Mama,
Trouble on my mind.
Lord, sweet Mama,
Trouble on my mind.
If you love me like you tell me,
Please, Mama, give a sign.

You know you hard on me,
Sometimes you act like you ain't there.
Even my daddy say you hard on me,
Say you act like you ain't there.
First you say you love me,
Then you don't act like you care.

I was dreamin an angel
When you called my name.
I had a dream about an angel
When you called my name.
Now I can't go back to sleep, Mama,
Nothin is the same.

I been layin here thinkin,
Now it's almost dawn.
I been layin here thinkin,
Now it's almost dawn.
If you won't turn my knees to jelly, Mama,
Let that sweet-talkin angel
I was dreamin about
Go on.

I woke up and wrote about it

Mel, I dreamed this,
and I woke up astounded.
The living room was flooded
with the afternoon's milky light.
I rose up out of sleep
like a woman drowned.
I walked around for weeks,
going to classes, cooking,
leading my ordinary life,
but I taught my friend Pamela
like a Kiowa dreamer
the song I had learned.

And all this time the universe
was inventing its perfect colors,
the changing sky was humming
its bleak and holy music.
All this time insects
were waking up
to their brief, meaningful lives,
snakes were writhing together
in the noisy leaves under the hedge.
All this time I was being born and dying
in every cell of my body,
the birds were singing,
the April grass
for the rest of the planet's life
was curled like billions of foetuses
on the delicate stairway
of this April's DNA.

And I am a part of this graceful rhythm
with you, my brother,
the only grown man now
who shares my genes.
This dream was a journey
into the lightest continent of my heart.
And like Jonah,
like the hermit who comes out of his cave,
like the mystic,
like the woman who prays,
I've come back empty-handed,
singing,
dazed.